Prepare to Meet Your Maker

Pearl Nsiah-Kumi

PREPARE TO MEET YOUR MAKER

Pearly Gates Publishing LLC
"Inspiring Christian Authors to BE Authors"

Pearly Gates Publishing LLC, Houston, Texas

Prepare to Meet Your Maker

Copyright © 2016
Pearl Nsiah-Kumi

All Rights Reserved.
No portion of this publication may be reproduced, stored in any electronic system, or transmitted in any form or by any means (electronic, mechanical, photocopy, recording, or otherwise) without written permission from the publisher. Brief quotations may be used in literary reviews.

ISBN 10: 1945117400
ISBN 13: 9781945117404
Library of Congress Control Number: 2016951114

For Information and bulk ordering, contact:
Pearly Gates Publishing LLC
Angela R. Edwards, CEO
P.O. Box 62287
Houston, TX 77205
BestSeller@PearlyGatesPublishing.com

Pearl Nsiah-Kumi

DEDICATION

To my beloved parents, the late James A. Sackar and the late Adolphine H. Okyerefo:
I look forward to reuniting with them in Heaven someday!

ACKNOWLEDGEMENT

Many thanks to my sister, Sheri D. Parmelee, Ph.D. Communication Studies, for her help with editing this book. Thank you, Sheri!

Pearl Nsiah-Kumi

INTRODUCTION

What is the "Book of Life"? The *Book of Life* is mentioned in the Book of Revelation, the last book of the Bible. The Bible warns there's a day coming when **everyone** will face God's judgment! Based on *His* verdict, some will go to Heaven - and others to Hell.

Are you ready? Where do you think you'll be going?

In the *Book of Life*, the names of all those who are going to spend eternity in Heaven are recorded. Don't you want to know ahead of time so you can avoid an unpleasant surprise? If you **do** want to know, you have to do what the Bible says.

There's only one way to get your name in that Book - regardless of your social status, education, gender, age, nationality, ethnicity, or education. The requirement is the same for each person! No one can bribe his or her way into Heaven.

The articles presented in this booklet explain what a person has to do to have his or her name recorded in the *Book of Life*, and thereby have the assurance in this life that he or she will go to **Heaven** after death.

Prepare to Meet Your Maker

TABLE OF CONTENTS

DEDICATION VI

ACKNOWLEDGEMENT VII

INTRODUCTION VIII

YOU BELONG TO ONE OF THESE FOUR GROUPS 1

GRACE PERIOD 7

IT IS POINTLESS AND NEEDLESS TO PERISH 11

DOES GOD EVER CHANGE HIS MIND? 15

HE EMPTIED HIMSELF OF ALL, EXCEPT LOVE 18

CHRISTIAN LIVING 21

HOW READILY-AVAILABLE IS YOUR ARMOR? 23

GOD'S APPEAL 25

CONCLUSION 28

YOU BELONG TO ONE OF THESE FOUR GROUPS

It is human nature to want to belong somewhere. Belonging to a group can be by choice or entitlement. For example, we don't **choose** our gender, ethnic groups, or the families we're born into. Those issues are beyond our control; however, we do get to decide who we want for friends, what professions we pursue, which associations we join, and which *other* groups appeal to us. Other times, we belong to a group based on our beliefs, likes, and dislikes.

For instance, when it comes to the issue of spirituality, each individual fits into one of four groups:

- People in **Group One** think they are good enough the way they are and will go to Heaven. In other words, they think they qualify to go to Heaven because they do enough good and are morally good people.

- People in **Group Two** think they are so sinful, God would want nothing to do with them. These people live under self-condemnation and hopelessness.

- **Group Three** believes they are sinners, but not beyond redemption. They understand from the Bible that Jesus died to pay for their sins. They have gratefully trusted Jesus with their sins and look forward to going to be with Him in Heaven when they die. In other words, they are Heaven-bound, but based only on God's grace and faith through Jesus - and not on anything they have done.

- People in the last group - **Group Four** - believe there is no God. They are called atheists.

For individuals in *Group One*, the Bible makes it clear that no one can get saved by obeying the law or being good. The Apostle Paul explains it this way: *"Now when a man works, his wages are not credited to him as a gift, but as an obligation. However, to the man who does not work but trusts God who justifies the wicked, his faith is credited as righteousness"* (Romans 4:4.5, NIV). No one is good 100% of the time and those who try to keep the law are unable to keep it 100% of the time. In addition, if salvation became available to us based on how **good** we were, it could be easy for us to boast about getting into Heaven on our own merit. Salvation, according to the Bible, is **only** by grace through faith.

You Belong to One of These Four Groups

For those in *Group Two* who think there is no hope for them, I have **excellent** news! God loves you so much, He's already made plans for you to be forgiven and restored to live a productive life **AND** for your name to be written in the *Book of Life*! He is willing and able to forgive your past - no matter how horrible. Consider the day Jesus was crucified: Two thieves were crucified as well, one on each side of Him. One thief asked for forgiveness. He petitioned Jesus to remember him when He got into His kingdom. Jesus forgave him and promised the thief that they would be together in paradise (see Luke 23:43). Similarly, there is hope for you! God is able to and will forgive you…if you repent.

The Israelites were in and out of favor with God so much because of their frequent unfaithfulness. To them He promised, "*Though your sins are like scarlet, they shall be as white as snow; though they are red like crimson, they shall be like wool*" (Isaiah 1:18, NIV). Your responsibility is to admit to God that, indeed, you are a sinner, ask for forgiveness, and accept His forgiveness. He will forgive and indwell you through His Spirit. You will then become a new creature because the Bible says, "*If anyone is in Christ, he is a new creation; the old has gone, the new has come!*" (2 Corinthians 5:17, NIV).

Pearl Nsiah-Kumi

The people in **Group Three** are the people whose names are written in the *Book of Life*. They are those who have placed their faith in Jesus. They understand that they cannot keep the law perfectly and that there is nothing they can do on their own to gain God's favor (see Isaiah 64:6). The grace of God has set them free from sin and Hell and, like the thief on the cross, they will be in Heaven with Jesus someday.

Although folks in **Group Four** - the atheists - believe there is no God, that belief **will not** change the fact that God **does** exist. It will also **not** excuse them from punishment for rejecting God. Contrary to the atheists' belief, the Bible says they do know God exists because "*The requirements of the law are written on their hearts, their consciences also bearing witness*" (Romans 2:15, NIV). This means deep down in an atheist's heart, there is that notion that God really does exists; he or she just chooses to believe otherwise.

So, which of these four groups can you *honestly* identify with? Have you trusted Jesus for salvation? If not, why not? What's holding you back?

You Belong to One of These Four Groups

You might belong in *Group One* - a good person, but God is not looking for 'good people'. He is looking for perfect people like Himself (see Matthew 5:48). You cannot be perfect until Jesus' righteousness is credited to you, and that comes only after you've placed your faith in Him. You cannot get into Heaven on your own merits!

If you are in *Group Two* - thinking you are hopelessly sinful - I invite you to try praying to God in Jesus' name. Ask Him to forgive you and make you His child - and He'll do that! You'll be amazed at the result! You'll never know until you take this step. You'll prove 2 Corinthians 5:17 to yourself **and** people who know you.

Free will is a gift from God, but our choices have consequences. We are each free to choose what we want to believe, whether we have facts to support it or not. Similarly, God has the right and the responsibility to honor **His** Word!

Jesus once announced to a crowd, "*Unless you repent, you, too, will all perish*" (Luke 13:3). Do you claim to be an atheist or an agnostic? **Please understand that your belief will not excuse you from God's wrath and judgment.** You need to rethink your position and put your faith in Jesus before it is too late.

Pearl Nsiah-Kumi

God is in the business of renewing, remaking, and restoring. Until you place your faith in Him, you are spiritually dead. Only He gives new life; avail yourself of that today!

GRACE PERIOD

The average person in our society is familiar with the expression "Grace Period". What does that mean? Grace period is the time period past a deadline that *could have* incurred some form of penalty for not fulfilling an obligation, but the penalty is waived.

An example would be where a professor expects an assignment to be turned in by a certain date, but permits students to turn it in a day or two later without penalty. Another example of a grace period would be in the arena of debt and payment due dates. Many companies assess and collect late fees if payment of a debt is not received by the agreed-upon due date. However, other companies do not impose the late fee for a few more days past the original due date, and that is the grace period.

Having explained the benefits of this concept in our **physical** world, let's see how it applies in the *spiritual* world.

Pearl Nsiah-Kumi

God is Holy, and therefore **hates** sin. He is also just, and therefore has to punish sin (see Romans 6:23). On the other hand, He loves us so much, He provided a substitute in the person of His Son, Jesus, who died in our place for our sins (see John 3:16). Hence, if we believe in Jesus, He forgives us and cleanses us from all unrighteousness (see 1 John 1:9).

God has a grace period as well in His dealings with us, our sins, and His relationship with us. Like the world, God's grace period has a limited window: It is between now (*the age of accountability*) and the day you die. In other words, you need to believe in Jesus while you are alive. No one can do that for you. If you die without believing in Jesus, you have chosen to forfeit salvation and accept God's judgment: ***Hell.*** The Bible says, "*Just as man is destined to die once, and after that to face judgment, so Christ was sacrificed once to take away the sins of many people; and He will appear a second time, not to bear sin, but to bring salvation to those who are waiting for Him*" (Hebrews 9:27-28, NIV).

Grace Period

Here are examples of people who either made good use of or missed the grace period:

- Noah's generation was so wicked, God decided to wipe out **every last one of them** - *except Noah*. God instructed him to build an ark for himself, his family, and the animals (see Genesis 6:1-22). Verse 22 says, *"Noah did everything just as God commanded him."* He would have perished with the rest of the world had he not followed God's instructions.

- The people of Sodom and Gomorrah were wicked as well. God decided to destroy the place; He sent two angels to go and accomplish that task! The angels decided to spare Lot - the **only** righteous man at the time - together with his wife, two daughters, and two future sons-in-law. They said to Lot, *"Do you have anyone else here - sons-in-law, sons or daughters, or anyone else in the city who belongs to you? Get them out of here, because we are going to destroy this place"* (Genesis 19:12-13, NIV). When Lot warned his sons-in-law, they did not leave because they thought he was joking (see Genesis 19:14). Those two men had the opportunity to escape destruction, but they missed it.

- Likewise, the people of Nineveh were a very wicked people. God sent Jonah to preach and warn them of pending judgment. He said to them, *"Forty more days and Nineveh will be overturned"* (Jonah 3:4, NIV). The Ninevites repented; they declared a fast for the whole city. Because they repented, God did not bring the destruction He had intended (see Jonah 3:10).

Whereas in the world, the duration of the grace period is the same across the board, the grace period in spiritual matters is not the same for all. The difference is because our lifespans vary; some live longer than others, but **your** grace period is over for you when you die or lose the ability to understand (as with poor health), no matter at what age. Procrastination is unwise and risky because we don't have the luxury of knowing ahead of time when the end will come. If we did, we could plan our day of salvation.

Have you believed in the name of Jesus? If you haven't, please be reminded: **Each day that passes brings you closer to the end of your grace period.** Call on the name of Jesus *today* and be saved!

IT IS POINTLESS AND NEEDLESS TO PERISH

You don't have to perish!

If you were hungry and a friend told you where you could find some food, would you listen or ignore the information and starve? How about the same scenario with thirst, nakedness, and illness? Would you pay attention? If you discovered a medication that was proven to cure whatever ails you, would you take it or would you rather suffer with that ailment and die? What would you do if you were cold and homeless, and someone offered you a warm home and warm bed? Would you choose to stay in the cold or accept the warm room and be comfortable?

I think the *average* person would answer "yes" to all of the above offers without hesitation. It makes no sense to suffer or die when help is available. Pain and death in the presence of help is **pointless** and **needless**.

Similarly, after God brought the Israelites out of captivity from Egypt, He made them an offer: He promised to be their God and Provider. He even promised to subdue their enemies. He simply asked that they listen to Him, submit to Him, follow His ways, and reject idols (see Psalm 81:8-14). Did they listen? **No!**

So, what did God do in response? He washed His hands of them and left them to their evil ideas. He said of them, "*I gave them over to their stubborn hearts to follow their own devices*" (Psalm 81:12, NIV). One might say that God said to the Israelites, **"Have it your way!"** It sounds very frustrating and heartbreaking, but since God has given man the power and ability to make choices, when man makes his own choices, God gets out of the way and allows man to face the consequences of his choices.

As the old adage goes, "*You make your bed, you lie in it.*"

It is Pointless and Needless to Perish

Before we belittle the Israelites for being stubborn or disobedient, I'd like to suggest that from the beginning of time, man has had this attitude - stubborn and disobedient! When Adam and Eve disobeyed God in the Garden, they lost their relationship with God. Years later, God revealed His plan to restore His relationship with man: In the person of Jesus, God became man and died as the substitute **for** man.

The only thing man must do is to admit to God that he is a sinner (*sin passed on to all men after the initial sin*) and ask God for forgiveness through His Son, Jesus Christ. The consequence of not believing in Jesus is **clearly** stated in the Bible. That consequence will be eternity in Hell, which is also referred to as the 'Lake of Fire' or the 'Second Death' (see Revelation 20:14).

You probably didn't know that truth before, but now that you do and now that you know the outcome of **not** believing in Jesus, don't you think you need to make the decision that will secure your future?

Pearl Nsiah-Kumi

Please don't argue about this. If you make the wrong choice, **it cannot be reversed later**. God loves you, but He will not *force* you to do anything against your will. Just as He left the Israelites to their own wicked devices, He will do the same with you.

Recently, there was an advertisement on television advocating separation of church and state. The character in the ad claimed to be an atheist. At the end of his presentation, he said, "I am an atheist, and I'll gladly go to Hell." How sad! *Does he know what it means to be in Hell?*

My heart ached for him, but then I became angry. Going to Hell is not something one should joke or be 'cute' about. Please don't let that man's attitude be your attitude, and please don't perish - because you really don't have to!

DOES GOD EVER CHANGE HIS MIND?

It is very natural for humans to change their minds about issues. We all change our minds from time to time about almost anything you can think of. We change our minds about decisions we've previously made and our stand on issues - political or otherwise. We also change our minds about our likes and dislikes, and anything else that's decision-worthy.

How about God? Doe He ever change His mind? The answer is "YES"!

That was probably **not** the answer you expected because you're likely thinking, "*God is all-knowing. Therefore, before He says anything, He already has His mind made up. For that reason, there should be no reason for Him to change His mind.*" I understand your reasoning, but yes; He does change His mind - in fact, He does so quite often!

You are probably thinking, **"NO WAY!"** So, why does He change His mind? What could *possibly* prompt the Almighty to change His mind? The answer is very simple: He changes His mind to prove His love for you and me, and to honor His promises to us.

Pearl Nsiah-Kumi

God's ability to change His mind is part of His love-nature! Based on His love for us, He has given Himself permission to change His mind, and that permission is written all over His commandments.

Under what circumstances, then, does God change His mind? He changes His mind in situations that call for punishment, but the sinner repents before the punishment is carried out. God changes His mind because He does not take **any** pleasure in the suffering or death of anyone (see Ezekiel 18:32). Rather, He demands and encourages repentance: "*Repent and live*", He says! For example, He tells us in Isaiah 55:7, "*Let the wicked forsake His way and the evil man his thoughts. Let him turn to the Lord, and He will have mercy on him, and to our God, for He will freely pardon*" (NIV). Also, in Romans 6:23, He says, "*The wages of sin is death*" - **BUT** if the sinner repents and puts his trust in Jesus, that death penalty is cancelled. Hence, the second half of that verse says, "*But the gift of God is eternal life through Christ Jesus our Lord.*"

Does God Ever Change His Mind?

Aren't you thankful that God is capable of changing His mind? I, for one, am **very** thankful because had He not changed His mind about me and my sins, my name would not be in the *Book of Life* - and He'll definitely have no place for me in Heaven. The alternative to that, of course, would be eternity in Hell. I encourage you to put your faith in Jesus Christ. Please understand that God's ability to change His mind concerning you will not benefit you in any way if you do not turn your life over to Him. He loves you so much that He sent His Only Son to die in your place. There is only one way to God, and that way is Jesus Christ, His Son. This is what Jesus claims: *"I am the way and the truth and the life. No one comes to the Father except through Me"* (John 14:6, NIV).

No matter how you've lived in the past, God is waiting for the opportunity to change His mind concerning you. He wants to give you the opportunity for a "makeover" in Christ. To assure you of that, He says, *"If anyone is in Christ, he is a new creation; the old has gone, the new has come"* (2 Corinthians 5:17, NIV).

Put your faith in Jesus **today** and be prepared to meet your Maker with assurance and confidence!

Pearl Nsiah-Kumi

HE EMPTIED HIMSELF OF ALL EXCEPT LOVE

Charles Wesley wrote very beautiful hymns during his life (1707-1788). One of my favorites is "Amazing Love", in which he emphasizes the mystery of Jesus' death. The third verse of that hymn goes like this:

"He left His Father's throne above - so free, so infinite His grace - Emptied Himself of all but love, and bled for Adam's helpless race [mankind]."

Jesus, being God, is immortal and has **all** power and **all** authority. For our sake, He temporarily and willingly gave up immortality, power, dignity, and authority. He washed His servants' feet and allowed Himself to be insulted, ridiculed, beaten, disrobed, and crucified; He died like a criminal, although He had done *nothing* wrong.

How many of our present-day leaders (kings, ministers, presidents, etc.) would accept anything less than what their positions allow them?

He Emptied Himself of All Except Love

Have you ever had an argument with someone who asked if you knew who he or she was? When people express themselves that way, they are really saying, **"I am a very important and powerful person. I deserve to be respected and don't you mess with me!"** Many people in positions of authority expect everybody else to recognize that - and respect them accordingly. They get highly indignant if they sense they've been denied that respect in *any* way.

Jesus, on the other hand, emptied Himself of everything - except love. Jesus' love for us and His obedience to His Father were His reasons for becoming flesh and dwelling among men. Love and obedience sent Him to the cross - and held Him there until He died! Had He allowed His immortality, power, authority, and the respect due Him to affect His decision, you and I would still be in our sins, unforgiven, and on the way to a Christless eternity. He emptied Himself of all - except love! *Have you taken advantage of this love?*

If you are an unbeliever, understand that Jesus died in your place. He gave up everything so He could die to save you. He died so you don't have to.

The Scripture puts it this way:

Pearl Nsiah-Kumi

"For God so loved the world that He gave His One and Only Son, that whoever believes in Him shall not perish but have eternal life. For God did not send His Son into the world to condemn the world, but to save the world through Him. Whoever believes in Him is not condemned, but whoever does not believe in Him stands condemned already" (John 3:16-18, NIV).

God wants you to respond to His sacrifice of love with a, **"Yes, Lord: I accept the death of your Son in my place. Please forgive my sins and make me your child."** The Bible tells us, *"If you confess with your mouth, 'Jesus is Lord', and believe in your heart that God raised Him from the dead, you will be saved"* (Romans 10:9, NIV).

On the other hand, if you are a Christian, you already understand salvation - but are you walking in humility and selflessness as Jesus walked? Jesus emptied Himself of all - except love. He instructs us: *"Let no debt remain outstanding, except the continuing debt to love one another, for he who loves his fellowman has fulfilled the law"* (Romans 13:8, NIV).

Yes, salvation is free, but it sure cost Him **everything**. For that reason, let's love Him through obedience. He said, *"Whoever has my commands and obeys them, he is the one who loves Me"* (John 14:21, NIV).

Christian Living

The Christian life is a transformed life; we have been moved from the Kingdom of Darkness into the Kingdom of Light. We cannot live this life without help - without the empowerment of the Holy Spirit who lives within.

Christians are adopted children of God. Prior to adoption, we were controlled by the devil. Each one of us had an earthly nature of sin, evidenced by sexual immorality, impurity, lust, evil desires, greed, anger, rage, malice, slander, and filthy language from the lips (see Colossians 3:6,8). Through the finished work of Christ, God rescued us from the devil's camp. This made us children of the Most High God. He put His Spirit into us to bear witness with our spirit that we really are His children and to teach us how to live godly lives.

As Christians, we are called to walk as Jesus walked. That means we turn our backs on sin, give up our former ways of living, and focus on God's ways. The Bible says that our lives are hid with Christ (see Colossians 3:3) - just as we might hide treasures from thieves. It is obvious that, if our lives are hid with Christ, we'll treasure His ways more than worldly ways.

Pearl Nsiah-Kumi

There are Christians who think believing in Jesus is all they need to do. They think that after they profess their faith, they are free to live any way that pleases them. In truth, believing in Jesus is only the **beginning** of the journey. Until we *see* Jesus face-to-face, we must continually seek to become more and more like Him. The Apostle Paul expresses it this way: *"Work out your salvation with fear and trembling"* (Philippians 2:12, NIV). John says it this way: *"We know that anyone born of God does not continue to sin"* (1 John 5:18), NIV). We need to make a conscious effort to hate sin and to have nothing to do with it.

It is clear from the Scriptures that God's wrath is coming against those who live in sin (see Colossians 3:6). Let us, therefore, keep ourselves clean. Our salvation cost Him a price we cannot imagine. The *least* we can do is live to please and honor Him.

How Readily-Available is Your Armor?

According to the Bible, Christians are in an ongoing warfare. It tells us, "*Our struggle is not against flesh and blood [humans], but against rulers, against the authorities, against the powers of this dark world, and against the spiritual forces of evil in the Heavenly realms*" (Ephesians 6:12, NIV).

This information is helpful because it calls us to be constantly prepared and ready to fight, implying we need gear - and a strategy. The Bible **also** says that, although we live in the world, we do not wage war like the world, and we do not employ the world's weapons (see 2 Corinthians 10:3-4). God has already won this struggle through Christ on the cross and provided protective gear to outfit us: The Armor of God (read Ephesians 6:10-18). He also tells us what our strategy should be and, in addition, He has demonstrated that the strategy works (see His response to His temptation - Luke 4:3-12)! **Amen!**

Pearl Nsiah-Kumi

We have a responsibility, though; the responsibility to put on the armor and keep it on, day and night. God does not do for us what we can and should do for ourselves. If we follow His direction, He will make sure we defeat the enemy in the battle.

The armor serves no purpose if we leave it hanging in the closet. **God does not put the armor on us and does not force us to put it on.** He does, however, make us aware of what the armor is, how to obtain it, and the importance of putting it on and keeping it on: *"So that you can stand against the devil's schemes"* (Ephesians 6:11, NIV).

Have you been defeated lately? Were you in your armor at the time? If you responded "Yes, I was", I seriously doubt that. So, where was your armor? Was it nicely tucked away in a suitcase or in your closet? It won't do you any good until you put it on and keep it on!

Victory on the battlefield is sure - **only** if we follow God's strategy. Let's have our armor on at *all* times!

GOD'S APPEAL

Our God is loving, just, and faithful. He does not play 'favorites'. As much as He longs for every soul to be saved, there are consequences for the unsaved. God will not change the rules for people who have not believed in the name of His Dear Son, Jesus. The Romans 6:23 pronouncement applies equally to all who do **not** believe: "*The wages of sin is death*" (NIV) - no matter who commits the sin. The end of the rich unbeliever is the same as the poor unbeliever. Likewise, the end of the unbelieving man is the same as the end of the unbelieving woman. Of course, God **could** make everyone believe in His Son, but He has given man the ability and the freedom to make *choices*. He wants man to love and obey Him by **choice** - not by force.

Since God longs so much to save the sinner, He has made us - His children - ambassadors to a sinful, dying world. Through us, He is appealing to the world to repent and come to salvation in Jesus Christ (see 2 Corinthians 5:20).

Synonyms for appeal include: *plead, petition, request, call, and demand.*

Pearl Nsiah-Kumi

It is almost as if God were *begging* people to come to salvation. Why would He go to the extent of **begging**? Well, because He knows what the end will be for unbelievers: Judgment. He yearns to see them escape that judgment. The Apostle Paul says, "*Knowing, therefore, the terror of the Lord, we persuade men*" (2 Corinthians 5:11, KJV).

So, what is our charge as Christian Ambassadors? Our charge is to let the **world** know that Jesus saves, and that God is making all things new in Christ Jesus who has already paid the penalty for our sins. We need to take His Word to *every* corner of the globe!

Man sinned, but God did not wait for man's apology (*in fact, I don't think man ever apologized*). Rather, God took the initiative to bridge the gap (the result of man's sin) between Him and man. What else can man **possibly** expect God to do? There is nothing left for God to do. The only acceptable restitution for sin has been made by Christ's sacrifice.

God's Appeal

So, let us *passionately* win souls for God. Our responsibility is to sow the seed, water it conscientiously with prayer, demonstrate it through godly living, follow up contacts when possible, and allow God to make it grow. Our responsibility *is not* to **force**, **shame**, or **scare** men to believe, but to reason with and persuade them.

Time is running out. The Lord is coming back soon. It could be too late for many.

Let us take our charge seriously, starting today! You came to faith through *someone's* efforts; it's **your** turn to help someone else come to faith.

God is appealing to your sphere of influence through you!

Pearl Nsiah-Kumi

CONCLUSION

Dear Reader,

It is my prayer and hope that these articles have encouraged you to place your faith in Jesus for salvation. It is important that you make this decision **now** rather than **later** - because later could be too late for you!

If you have placed your faith in Jesus, **welcome** to the family of God! Now, seek out your siblings (*other Christians*) and fellowship with them so you can be encouraged in your faith. Seek to know the Word of God through daily Bible reading and prayers.

May God bless you in your walk as you seek to obey His Word.

Lastly, don't forget to share your faith with others because Jesus died for them as well.

Pearl

www.ingramcontent.com/pod-product-compliance
Lightning Source LLC
Chambersburg PA
CBHW071549080526
44588CB00011B/1839